CELEBRATING FAILURE

CELEBRATING FAILURE

DHRUV AVDHESH

Notion Press

Old No. 38, New No. 6
McNichols Road, Chetpet
Chennai - 600 031

First Published by Notion Press 2017
Copyright © Dhruv Avdhesh 2017
All Rights Reserved.

ISBN 978-1-947586-26-0

While every effort has been made to trace copyright holders (if any) and obtain permissions, this has not been possible in all cases. Any omissions brought to the attention of the Author will be remitted in future editions. No part of this book shall be used, reproduced in any manner whatsoever without written permission from the author, except in the case of brief quotations embodied in critical articles and reviews.

The Author of this book is solely responsible and liable for its content including but not limited to the views, representations, descriptions, statements, information, opinions and references ["Content"]. The Content of this book shall not constitute or be construed or deemed to reflect the opinion or expression of the Publisher or Editor. Neither the Publisher nor Editor endorse or approve the Content of this book or guarantee the reliability, accuracy or completeness of the Content published herein and do not make any representations or warranties of any kind, express or implied, including but not limited to the implied warranties of merchantability, fitness for a particular purpose. The Publisher and Editor shall not be liable whatsoever for any errors, omissions, whether such errors or omissions result from negligence, accident, or any other cause or claims for loss or damages of any kind, including without limitation, indirect or consequential loss or damage arising out of use, inability to use, or about the reliability, accuracy or sufficiency of the information contained in this book.

Praises for the Author

"Learning from failure is not a new philosophy. It's as old as they come. Dhruv Avdhesh, however, has taken the idea a step further and wants people to celebrate failure, which is something he thinks he did too. Sounds like a philosopher? Or any other inspirational speaker? Dhruv, at the ripe young age of 20, is but a college student whose voice, by the sound of it, hasn't even cracked yet."

– **The New Indian Express**

"The quality that I really admire about Dhruv is his intellectual curiosity and inquisitiveness. He doesn't only ask thought provoking questions, but also wants to be a part of the solutions. Apart from being blessed with a fine persona, Dhruv has built in him an armor of technical prowess that enables him to add values to organizations in more ways than one. It won't be wrong to say that he matured faster than some of his peers and has a bright future ahead of him."

– **Rachit Khosla**, Founder, Conquerem

Praises for the Author

"An extremely sharp go-getter with a sound technical knowledge. Vivacious and charismatic with a focused, intelligent, analytical, objective and practical approach makes him a potent combination. Keep it up."

– **Mohak Mahajan**, Operations Head, Order Gifts Online

"Dhruv not only does what he loves, but he is amazing at it. His commitment, passion, knowledge of the field are a few great things about him and his work. He has fresh ideas and I am glad to have met him."

– **Priya Taneja**, Founder, The Calling Chits

"Dhruv, once again - congrats and pat yourself on the back. It's super stuff!"

– **Nehha Bhatnagar**, Founder & Director, Sarvam Foundation

"Well done Dhruv. You must know that given your potential, you have a long way to go. Though it's been a great start! Will be happy to be a part of all your learning and success. Hugs!"

– **Kamal Seth**, Founder & Chief Happiness Officer, Human Circle

Praises for the Author

"I found him to be sincere, diligent and committed in his efforts. His ability to innovate combined with good communication skills added to the quality of work."

– Shubhendra Nigam,
Chief Organizer, Cross Model United Nations

"I found him to be sincere and hard working."

– Devendar Kumar Bansal,
Director, Bansal Handicrafts

"We found him to be motivated, hardworking and a self-starter. We appreciate all his efforts."

– Dhruv Jain, Founder, Print Octopus

"Dhruv has played an important role in spreading the message of social action against the youth. He has shown exceptional leadership skills, dedication and hard work."

– Uma Parvathy, General Manager,
Leaders for Tomorrow

"Dhruv is a great designer and always makes it a point to deliver work in time."

– Sagar Tamboli,
Co-Founder, Documendz

Praises for the Author

"Oh my god. You just made my day. I don't really know if I can ever repay anything you do for me. And nothing will give you enough justice, not even the words I try to write for you."

– **Sonakshi Kothary**

"Key advantages of working with Dhruv have been commitment to time, development update methodology, understanding aesthetics from different point of views, and ability to adjust the available technology to suit our needs into the best possible way."

– **Prateek Sood**, Director, Grand Slam Fitness

"Smooth and reliable."

– **Puneet Malhotra**, Co-Founder, Follow Your Sport

"His attention to detail, explanation of various technical aspects and working according to a timeline are just a few of his talents showcasing commitment to his work."

– **Arjun Mehta**, Chief Business Development Officer, Naina Semiconductor Limited

Dedication

"It is said that if you end up with a boring, miserable life because you listened to your mom, your dad, your teacher, your priest or some guy on television telling you how to do your stuff, then you deserve it!"

Dedicated to the #DoWhatYouLove Movement, to my nation, my parents and my heavenly brother.

Contents

	Prologue	xiii
1.	Glass Ceiling in the Gentleman's Club (Anupama Joshi)	1
2.	A Little *Qtiyapa* Never Hurt Anyone (Arunabh Kumar)	9
3.	Dance to Dignity (Nehha Bhatnagar)	18
4.	Of Artistry in a Sand Grain (Rahul Arya)	27
5.	The Piper's Tune (Archy Jay)	37
6.	Living *Asimov's* Dream (Diwakar Vaish)	47
7.	Turn up the Torque (Alisha Abdullah)	56
8.	The Notes and Rhythm of Perseverance (Varun Rajput)	61
9.	Blue Streak (Mithali Raj)	70

10.	The Tree of Knowledge (Kunal Arora)	81
	Epilogue	*87*
	References	*95*
	Acknowledgement	*97*
	Contributors	*101*
	About the Author	*103*

Prologue

"It is impossible to live without failing at something, unless you live so cautiously that you might as well not have lived at all – in which case, you fail by default."

– Joanne K. Rowling

The goal behind writing this book is very simple. By the means of this book, I am trying to break stereotypical mind-sets prevalent in our society and what could have been better than sharing stories of ten sung and mostly unsung people who celebrated failure by doing what they loved.

So, what actually is 'failure'?

In the simplest way, failure (/ˈfeɪljə/) is defined as the lack of success or the state or condition of not meeting a desirable or intended objective.

True, that might sound as the perfect definition for failure; but the idea of failure is much, much more than that. In today's fast paced world, failure is considered something very derogatory. Students in schools and colleges are punished for failing in examinations, corporates are fired from their companies for not meeting their targets, divorced women are still not allowed to enter places of worship, lovers commit suicide after a broken relationship, people give up on their dreams after being bankrupt, are just a few examples or perceptions of failures.

People who fail at something are generally seen with disrespectful eyes and are treated with vituperative behaviour. Failure in our times has been so negatively over-emphasized that people nowadays are even scared to fail—so much so that people do not even try to achieve or reach their goals that they wanted to, in the initial place, which is even worse as quoted by J.K. Rowling... and that, my friend, is actual failure.

Failure comes with its own emotional baggage which is not easy to let go off. According to the World Health Organization (WHO), India is one of the most depressed countries in the world with a whooping thirty-six per cent (more than one-third) of Indians are likely to suffer from major depression at some point in their lives. I am not a psychologist or a psychiatrist, but been there and having done that, I can totally state with my utmost belief and without an iota of doubt that the cause of any kind of depression or feelings of sadness or remorse is the chemical reactions that go on in our brain when we are anxious to fail. Let us all ask ourselves what is that one thing that stops us from performing to the best of our potential today? I guarantee you that there would have been a faint internal voice that told you that you feared failing in something and if you failed, then the world would judge you, your family, your friends, your teachers, your boss, etc.

Before going any further, I would like to share a personal story from my journal, which has been archived for a while now, but is important to mention now because this one incident largely shaped who I am today.

First year (II semester) was about to end and I was looking for a summer internship frantically. I met this guy (who later became my boss) on LetsIntern.com who had just started a new company. We exchanged a few emails and I was called for an interview at Burbee's Café in Sector 18, Noida, Uttar Pradesh, India. I cleared the interview and was appointed as a Tech Intern. He was really thrilled after seeing my website at that point of time. An official agreement was signed within a week's time. All was set and the internship began on a good note.

To start with, we were a team of three interns – A backend PHP developer, a marketer and me (the front-end and user interface developer). Within two or three weeks, the front end of the website and the user interface of the mobile application was completed and handed over. At this point of time, my marketer colleague was sacked for reasons not known to me and the company officially began its operations around this time. During this time, I had also set up their social media handles and within the next one week, I also made their blogging website. By the end of the first month, I received a mail from the Chief Executive Officer (CEO) of the company (in my case, my immediate boss), that he no longer found me motivated enough to work from office as I had denied his order to stay after 6 pm in the office (even when the day began at 9 am).

Soon, we two remaining interns were given a holiday of one week with some homework to do. Within this week, I had to come up with the front-end of a brand new website that would replace the old one and make a marketing video and a presentation to be shown to potential investors. The work was completed and submitted before time. By the time we returned to office, we were informed that the company had failed to make its mark and soon the operations would be closed. Another week in office, I was asked to make the graphical user interface of a new mobile application as the business was now being shifted to Dubai with a complete new idea that was miles apart from the initial one.

As I was returning home from office one day, my boss called on my landline number, which my mom answered and then later he called me on my mobile as I was still in the metro to inform me that my internship had been terminated and I did not need to come to office from the next day. I did not tell my mom that something like this had happened, but when I told her later, she just said that she already knew about it as he had called on the landline.

On the same day, the official website was brought down, the mobile application deleted from Google Play Store, social media handles deactivated and a public announcement was made through text messages that the company was shutting down the next day and that they'd be back soon. The drama and subsequent suffering had just begun.

As soon as I reached home, I called my boss to discuss with him that what went wrong and why he was so angry. He deliberately did not take my calls and replied with a message instead that read: "Dhruv, let's not play a blame game here. Both I and ****** have tried our absolute best with you. We'll definitely meet sometime. But you know how busy I keep. We'll surely try to meet up in first week of August."

I was so horrified that I called the other co-founder who is also the tech lead of the company and he told me that he was shocked to know that something like this had happened. He asked me to meet him in office the next day to resolve the issue. Though the co-founder had just left his corporate job, my bond with him was stronger than that with the CEO as he would help me in tech problems that I had faced while trying to understand new things. The co-founder did meet me and told me that he would speak to the CEO as he did not have any problem with my work. That day, the meeting went for more than two hours and I left the office crying. Next morning when I woke up, I found a mail in my inbox saying that my internship was terminated last week and the following are the reasons for the same:

- I was using my talent in his office on some other organization's project.
- I haven't produced the expected results at work.
- I create constant disturbance in the office that leads to low productivity.

I was thrown out of my first full-time office-based internship for totally unacceptable reasons to me. What you just read here is a small part of the complete story, what followed was even more disturbing. But the question here is not who was right or wrong. The fact, till date, remains the same that I failed in something that I truly loved doing and that too when my parents had warned me against the same.

I was left shattered and a feeling of self-doubt had begun to sink in. I was left abandoned in my thought process and I could hardly express how I felt. But the only thing I knew was that there was more to learn and experience. I did not give up and today, I have developed twenty-two websites, successfully completed seven internships, held six positions of responsibilities, and in total have completed, a little over thirty projects (still counting).

It's just not me who has been through such low times but all of us face such situations regularly in our lives, but that does not mean that we should give up. Failure is something inevitable; if we want to achieve something in life than we have to exponentially increase our failure rate. As Bill Gates once said, "It's fine to celebrate success but it's more important to pay heed to the lessons of failure." Success is something passive whereas failure is something that invokes an action.

What follows next are the true mind-boggling life stories of people who celebrated failure by doing what they loved; and while doing so, made a dent in the universe. The following people's narrative awaits you:

- Anupama Joshi (First female Wing Commander of the Indian Air Force)
- Arunabh Kumar (Founder and The Chief Experiment Officer, The Viral Fever Media Labs)

- Nehha Bhatnagar (Youngest arts impresario in India)
- Rahul Arya (India's first sand artist)
- Archy Jay (India's first female bagpipe artist)
- Diwakar Vaish (Creator of India's first dancing robot, India's first 3D-printed robot, India's first mind-controlled robot and the world's first brain controlled wheelchair)
- Alisha Abdullah (India's first female national racing champion)
- Varun Rajput (Founder, producer and guitarist, Antariksh)
- Mithali Raj (Captain, Indian female cricket team)
- Kunal Arora (Founder, The Education Tree)

For those who have an open mind for new ideas, who seek to create long lasting success, I offer you a challenge. From now on, start celebrating failure!

#CelebrateFailure

Glass Ceiling in the Gentleman's Club

It was way back in 1992 that the government of India opened its door for women to join the armed forces and Wing Commander Anupama Joshi was the first female Wing Commander of the esteemed Indian Air Force (IAF). She says, "To tell you the truth, the glamour of the uniform was not the only thing, but the feel to rough it out in the frontiers was my calling."

Twenty-five thousand women applied to be a part of the elite force and she was fortunate enough to be one of the pioneers. The adrenaline rush and the pride she got when she donned the uniform for the first time was something phenomenal.

She was thrown into the Air Force Academy with a grilling schedule. The day would start with a run and before she knew it, she would be on a parade, drill, cross-country weapon training and jungle training in the middle of the night. It was the Air Force way of indoctrinating the new recruits.

Many lessons were learned by her, but the prime being—when you are asked to jump you do not ask why, you just ask how high. Donning her blues with pride and glory she reported to the first place of her posting and she walked down the corridors of the officer's mess and asked the mess in charge, "Where is the room key for pilot officer Joshi? He looked at her rather quizzically and responded, "Where is the officer?" Wing Commander Joshi cheerfully remarked, "I cannot tell you the incredulous look on his face when I told him I was the officer." It really struck her then that men were not prepared to accept women as officers and she was soon to realise that he was not the only one. It's not about crafting a narrative here, but the ground reality.

She felt like being watched all the time. The seniors wouldn't know how to treat her—whether she was a lady or a junior officer. Her colleagues would be sitting in a dining hall that would be packed with laughter and energy; and suddenly there would be pin drop silence the moment she walked in because they didn't know how to socially react to a female officer. Every minute and every time, she was treated more as a woman, less as an officer.

Once, she faced an incident of insubordination which was unheard of in a military establishment. When a man placed under her refused to take orders and when she complained, it was she who was counselled, saying that the man in question belonged to a state where he was socially engineered to not to take orders from a woman. It was then she realised; and many such incidents made her realise that though opportunity was given, there were a huge amount of barriers that needed to be broken and a massive mindset to be changed.

And if I may add, it has taken the Indian Air Force twenty years to actually break the sound barrier when they finally accepted a woman in a combat role and now we have a frontline fighting force. However, there is a long-drawn history of legal battles and that's where Wing Commander Joshi's story begins.

So, when the euphoria of the induction of women was over, the reality hit her because then she realised that women as a whole did not have the right entitlement—be it for it was courses, promotions, posting, placements. Women were inducted initially for five years and they were not given permanent positions because IAF kept saying that they were in an 'experimental zone.'

As Wing Commander Joshi was nearing the completion of her first engagement, she put up a representation asking why women should not be given a permanent place like their male counterparts. She did not hear anything from them, but suddenly after seven months, she was given an extension of four years. "Brilliant!"

Life moved on and she admits that the life in military is something very amazing. As she was coming close to her second tenure, she represented again, asking about career prospects for women in the armed forces. Silence prevailed and she did not hear from them for long. Long after, she got a reply informing her that it was a matter of tri-services because the Army and Navy were also involved and the matter was lying with the Ministry of Defence. She waited for the answer... a year passed, but no reply came her way.

She put her third application requesting for an interview with the Chief of the Air Staff. He said the same thing, "Anupama... wait... the matter is with the Ministry of Defence..." and wait is what she did.

One year passed; she put her next application and by then the Chief had changed. The new Chief had taken over and she still got no reply; but she got a six-year extension into the service. But that wasn't very exciting for her. What kept annoying her, and the source of all her anger is this ad hoc treatment. The question kept hounding her as to why women couldn't get a permanent place and why women couldn't fully continue their tenure. Why does a woman not have the choice to serve their country, which is their constitutional right?

Not giving up, she forwarded another application, this time to the Supreme Commander of the Armed Forces that is the honourable President of India. That application did not see the light of the day. So, she wanted to move forward. By then, it was already six applications and six years had gone by.

She put up an application under the Right to Information (RTI) Act and her RTI application was stone-walled, quoting that that the matters of human resource establishment in the military is of national importance and does not fall under the ambit of RTI.

What was she left to do? Knock at the doors of the court. By then, a large number of women had already joined the forces. She went ahead and contacted many of them, so that they could do a collective representation and it could become a class ace, but only one came forward. She went to the court with a very simple prayer that women should be given a permanent place in the Indian

Air Force on the basis of their efficiency and not on the basis of their gender.

She explains, "You must understand that this was a very daunting task for me because I was fighting against an organisation which is extremely structured, hierarchical and disciplined."

Three years in the corridors of Delhi High Court, she found her success; and it was in 2010 that the landmark judgement came that women would be given permanent places in the Armed Forces.

You may have the courage; you may have the conviction but it is the perseverance that shall prevail. For Wing Commander Joshi, there were lots of lessons taught in the classroom that came in handy; and as the Chinese military strategist Sun Tzu said in his *Art of War* was that you must make your war into a crusade, it shouldn't be about oneself and it should be about a group. Only then shall victory come from the most unexpected quarters, and she happily acknowledges that in the battle for equal opportunity, the larger support came from men. The men who inducted her, the superiors and colleagues who believed in her and the judges were all men.

She was re-instated into the service and it's a historical moment in the Indian Armed Forces. She did not join for personal reasons but it Is important to know that the battle was for equal opportunity and she expresses that being a soldier is not only about courage; it's about sacrifice too. Also, do not ever try to teach a woman that.

Working hard to clear a path for others so that they can confidently go on to do bigger and better things has in turn inspired others to clear a path for Wing Commander Joshi to do exactly the same thing. As a woman in the very masculine world of the military, she has set a great example by not giving up to the fears and failures that came in her path and hence she has made her mark in the history of the Armed Forces and India. Great leadership is not about flexing muscle or power and intimidation. Great leaders as she embody a sense of purpose that inspires those around them. Generations of women will remember her as a true leader and a soldier who fought for their rights in this unjust world where women are seen as inferior beings.

A Little *Qtiyapa* Never Hurt Anyone

The Chief Experiment Officer (CEO) of The Viral Fever (TVF) Media Labs – Arunabh Kumar was brought up in the small town of Muzzafarpur in Bihar. He was schooled all over India and when his parents didn't like his school they would simply change it. Arunabh's strict disciplinarian dad made him appear for the Joint Entrance Examination; and sadly, he couldn't clear it in the first attempt. Later, he was sent to Kota in Rajasthan for preparing for the exams and he made it through the Indian Institute of Technology (IIT), Kharagpur, in the next attempt.

From being a guitarist to a civil services aspirant to being a full-time research consultant at Accenture and the United States Air Force, he had pretty much thought and tried everything before he finally quit his job to give India what we today popularly known as TVF. But the journey was not either easy or smooth. The struggle was real. There were days when Arunabh didn't even have the money to pay the rent.

Even his first video *Engineer's Diary* was rejected by MTV and other popular youth-centric channels. What followed afterwards made TVF and Arunabh Kumar a household name.

Here is the famous electrical engineer in his own words:

On Being an IITian

"When I finally made it to IIT Kharagpur, I thought college would be like the one in *Kuch Kuch Hota Hai*. But it was nothing like how I thought it would be. It was a fuck all college. I actually ran away; but, I had to go back and complete my degree. What's best about having a degree from IIT is the fact that you make really good friends. I have friends in a lot of cities and they were well earning, they helped me out with my expenses when I needed it the most. You obviously stand to benefit if you're from an IIT. People think you are smart, they trust you. The perception and trust is the asset an IIT alumnus has."

On Failing in Exams

"I failed in seven subjects in the first year and five in the second year. I mulled over about fifteen to seventeen career options before I zoned in on passionately following theatre in the third year of college."

On Rote Learning

"I genuinely believe that nothing ever comes from rote learning. It is very important that you use your own brain."

On Dropping Out of College

"I am all for education. I think it is not necessary for you to drop out of college in order to follow your dreams. Dropping out of college has become a fashionable thing to do, when or if you drop out. When you are sure about yourself and your plans, then you're not quitting or dropping out but moving onto something better."

On Career Choices

"Every semester I used to pick a different career choice in the first semester, I wanted to be an economist in the second semester I wanted to do a Masters in Business Administration (MBA); and in the third, I thought I would be a coder;

and in the fourth semester I thought I would join the Union Public Service Commission (UPSC)."

On Students from Other Colleges

"I'm sure students from not-so-famous colleges are probably much smarter than the ones studying in IIT. At the end of the day, it all comes down to how hard you work that decides how well you'll do in life."

On the Current Day Youth

"When I meet juniors today, I find them really impatient. They want to do things quickly. It took me four years to figure out whether or not I wanted to enter the industry. It takes time to understand how things work especially because the world around us is extremely complex. Investing time is essential. Our entire generation is not into television; most of us don't watch it. I wanted to make India's version of *The Big Bang Theory* and *FRIENDS*."

On Education

"I consider Red Chillies Entertainment to be my film school and all these guys—Shah Rukh Khan, Farah Khan and all the technicians were my teachers. Most of my media and filmmaking education happened with these guys and I am fortunate to work with them."

On Entrepreneurship

"For an entrepreneur, there's this popular saying that goes something like, 'You are your own boss,' but I think we need to change this around a little. According to me, you are never your own boss but always your own employee because you have to work at least ten to fifteen hours."

On Quitting his Job

"I was at the airport, about to take a flight to Tokyo. They had just announced boarding and that was it. I got up; but instead of heading to boarding, I headed out of the airport. It all happened rather serendipitously because of an article in the Times of India about a certain Arunabh Kumar who quit his job to pursue his dream; My Dad, who had read about it, called me immediately."

On Money

"Nobody gave me even one fucking rupee!"

On Rejection

"Luckily, Canon camera, YouTube and my rejection came at the right time; all three of them coincided. This *College Qtiyapa* is a show I had conceived for MTV. That show too got rejected after a lot of resources went into it. That was one of the best rejections in my life; else we wouldn't have *Qtiyapa* with us. I had started doing branded content and my scripts were getting rejected a lot."

On Naysayers

"They too were suffering from the same creative inertia. These were the kinds of people who would sit in the confines of their comfortable spaces in Bandra and talk about the Indian youth."

On Creative Feudalism

"There are 1.2 billion people in the country and twenty people cannot just know what should be made. Raghu Ram from the TV show *Roadies* was not even allowed to audition for some of the channels; I was very angry with the approach they had. I had made smaller videos on a smaller scale, which were loved by three-thousand people in my college and I believed that three-thousand people each in a thousand colleges around the country too would like it, which makes it thirty-lakh people. So, I truly believe that there are three million people waiting to watch this stuff."

"There are about fifty people in film, and around twenty in television who get to decide what would be made."

On his Dad

"My Dad has watched only one movie his entire life. He's someone who believes that films, television serials and music belong to the devil."

On Creativity

"Unfortunately in India, when someone says creativity, everyone thinks of Bollywood."

"The idea was to do something new; but, that wasn't welcome in the industry."

On Experimentation

"We kept experimenting. I never asked clients how much money they would give me, but they would never ask me what I was making—that was the deal."

On Making Web Series

"When I decided to create a drama-based web series; it was pretty scary initially. These were twenty-minute-long videos and they only existed at TVF in India."

On Acting Himself

"My journey from behind the camera to in front of it has not been easy because I feel acting is one of the toughest jobs in the world and one needs to be very intelligent to constantly do that. Good acting is completely opposite to the notion that anyone can act. In fact, in India, very few people know this art. I think they could not find another balding and aged actor to play the role and that's why I was selected. It's a character that is very strong and some fans have compared it to Ari Gold from the show *Entourage*. But personally, I would call it a *Dabanng* in a corporate office or in a start-up. It's rare that we see or deal with characters that are real and quirky and belong to the new India; and this is the reason why people have related with us."

On Success

"I can officially say that TVF is bigger than MTV—in terms of manpower, scale, amount of original content and brand value. That naïve, stupid dream has come true."

On Future Plans

"We don't smoke up and think of ideas. We actually want to be like a HBO or Disney, and so we work towards it. Maybe, we will be the Disney of India after all."

On Defying the Odds

"I think it's folks like us who come up with the different ideas because we really have no other choice but to break the mould. Today, we can't imagine our lives without *Pitchers*, *Permanent Roommates*, *Barely Speaking with Arnub* and other TVF shows, videos and songs. What one random Arunabh started years ago from his bedroom and make-shift office, has now become one of the only online Indian channels worth watching today. He successfully converted his dreams in to reality and passion in to paychecks by doing what he loved.

TVF had gathered two thousand subscribers, eighteen million views and less than forty uploaded videos in just eighteen months. Today, Arunabh has booked his berth in the *Fortune* Top 40 under 40 list for 2015 and 2016. He was also included in *GQ*'s list of Most Influential Young Indians for 2015 and 2016. His widely-appreciated online series *Pitchers* is currently rated #27 and *Permanent Roommates* is rated #162 on IMDB's Top Rated Television Shows.

Dance to Dignity

Nehha was born into a family of two ever-hungry dachshunds, an ambitious mom, a super punctual dad, a naughty brother and a whole bunch of loving aunts and uncles and grandparents. An aspirational middle-class family, Nehha's parents put her brother Jay and her in Delhi's foremost liberal arts focused school—The Shri Ram School in Gurgaon, Haryana, where you weren't allowed to take back any homework with you. Her school life was spent in a most creative way—from editing newspapers, painting, clay pottery, volleyball, national-level roller hockey, classical dance lessons, swimming, vocal music classes and more. Every creative activity worth trying out was tried out and the mother would usually spend hours on the road driving the children from one class to the other! Holidays were spent making projects by hand or joining the Captain father at sea or travelling to the hills, bag and baggage with the jingbang of cousins in tow!

The final two years of school were spent at a more academically-oriented school—the hard taskmaster called Delhi Public School, Vasant Kunj. Nehha, a student of the Humanities stream performed her first solo Bharatanatyam show under her former Guru, right before her final board exams! But then, when her exam results came out, she had stood first all-India in three subjects and also topped in Delhi, and obviously, in her school in the Humanities stream.

When asked about how she used to manage so much at a time, she happily expressed, "If you can't challenge yourself, you can't do multiple things."

Nehha walked into the prestigious Lady Shri Ram College, Delhi University for Sociology Honors, but later transferred her credits to a Knox College, a liberal arts college in Illinois, USA, for an undergraduate degree in International Relations to be next to her boyfriend. Knox had a great diversity, which opened up her horizons and Nehha believes that the American system of education challenges an individual, both academically and emotionally. It was at Knox that Nehha truly realized where her forte lies—in being a cultural ambassador for India. Her mind opened up to cultures from around the world and she saw the unique position India's culture held in their eyes.

Post graduating, Nehha joined a new Guru, the legend Dr. Saroja Vaidyanathan (choreographer and exponent of Bharatanatyam) in Delhi. Simultaneously, she also enrolled in a Masters program at Delhi University for Political Science with a focus in International Relations. She began her cultural tours with the dance troupe at her Guru's school. The performances began and how! From Kazakhstan to Shillong, Nehha's tryst with Bharatanatyam truly blossomed. She began to be invited for giving TEDx talks and the idea of teaching dance to underprivileged girls took root through these talks. Nehha began training girls from a nearby slum at a non-governmental organization (NGO) called Nai Disha Educational and Cultural Society.

In 2009, Nehha had simultaneously begun an internship with the then Minister for External Affairs Dr. Shashi Tharoor's office. Writing and researching in politics gave her insight into the working of her field of study. She would also learn, through the course of her association with Dr. Tharoor, the importance of shaping soft-power diplomacy.

Nehha combined her dance with diplomacy to give rise to a form of artistic expression and human interaction that can be called 'Dance Diplomacy,' which helped her build deeper bonds with a lot of dignitaries and diplomats. This was also the time when she broke up with her boyfriend due to time commitment issues. Of course, that break up did take a toll on her since both of them had been in a seriously committed relationship for a few years and had already dreamt of being married someday.

In 2010, she was invited by TEDx Pune to speak on the topic *Dance to Dignity*. The response the talk received made her quite a special speaker in the TEDx community in India. Soon after, in April 2012, Nehha quit the office of Dr. Shashi Tharoor to make a larger and deeper impact.

Later that year, a spark of sorts struck. Nehha hosted her first TEDx Tughlaq Road event to give a stage to lesser-heard voices. Seeing the success of the collaboration, she began organising new themes and out-of-the-box ideas for the arts. There was a dire need for creating a new audience for classical arts. And this is what Nehha aimed to do with her organisation. As she saw more and more people connect with her work and newer faces turning up for the collaborations she showcased along with new artistes, the name of the organisation seemed clearer to her. *Sarvam* the

Sanskrit name means 'all encompassing' and is also an acronym for Saroja Vaidyanathan Arts Mission.

For arts to truly thrive and survive, both in terms of artistes and audience, Nehha began *Sarvam* Foundation in 2012 to provide a fresh perspective to the performing arts of India; Not excluding anyone, but instead taking everyone along with her—be it the underprivileged girl child or the usually busy corporate chief executive officers.

During this journey, Nehha was selected by Rotary International to go on a scholarship to Macau, China. When she came back, she started a residency program with Rama Vaidyanathan (fellow Bharatanatyam dancer and daughter-in-law of Saroja Vaidyanathan) to re-inculcate the feeling of *Gurukul* (residential schools in India) in Zorba the Buddha in Delhi. Hundreds of new dancers from across the globe started pouring in for the program. Even artists from Pakistan, who usually don't get visas very easy, started participating in the residency program in great numbers.

Nehha is of the point of view that she had a not-so-famous Guru to begin with and therefore, did not get enough opportunities initially. She says that she didn't get a stage to perform in her childhood and therefore she thought of creating opportunities for herself and for others like her. She adds that there was no respect in taking up a career in the field of arts till a few years ago. Dancers weren't provided a green room and even the stage was not up to the mark and usually had dangerous protrusions from the floor that could hurt anybody during a performance.

Now, a new paradigm in arts, *Sarvam,* has quite humbly created classical dance history; and now, the situation has started improving and people have started giving respect to artists.

Nowadays, Nehha realises that she has done so much that is not possible for every individual. She thinks that she has a divine ordinance and hence, she has been sent to Earth to be a medium for the arts. She reveals that during one of her first self-curated events at Kamani Auditorium in Delhi, there was a gathering of eight-hundred people and she was the sole person running the show. She literally had no funding but still she was able to put up a great show as everything fell in place on its own. This helped her faith to grow and never let the success get to her head. Soon, she was interviewed on DD Bharati for the same.

Nehha has single-handily curated, conceptualized and empowered various events. Along the journey, many amazing people have lent their support. And many are continuing to do so, but her personal life has not been less than a rollercoaster ride.

After the break up with her boyfriend who she wanted to marry, she was single for more than eight or nine years, which wasn't as simple as it may sound. All this was happening because she wasn't able to take out time from her cultural activities; and the pressure to get married and get settled was building up from her mom's end. A lot of people started visiting her with marriage proposals but almost all of them would turn her down saying that they can marry an entrepreneur who works for herself but can't marry a dancer as it was below the dignity of their family and the society to which they belonged to. Nehha, on hearing such comments, would feel bitter and was left destroyed each time.

Recently, in December 2015, she fell really sick and thought of slowing down. At this point she began thinking on what's next in life. This was when she got in a relationship with one of her old friends, which ended a few days ago due to the same reason of time commitment from her side. She again started doubting and questioning herself as girls of her age were already married or getting there. She even started looking out for her 'better half' on matrimonial sites.

But today, she happily voices that she could have gone home with a bag full of things except for dreams and that a lot of marriages are ending on sore notes or most of them aren't happy since they do not share a common passion or understanding.

But the other side of the coin is that Nehha is doing what she loves. She believes in herself and in her dance and is no longer scared of failing at stupid marriage proposals or heartbreaks from petty relationships that were never supposed to work. For her, dance is the celebration of life and the groom she is supposed to marry will reveal himself in due course of time.

Her project for the girls from the slums of Delhi has grabbed a lot of eyeballs not only in India but across the globe. *Sarvam*'s yearly calendar is the largest art calendar in the world. Recently, she was invited to be a part of Milapfest, the United Kingdom's leading South Asian Art Festival in Liverpool.

Sarvam Foundation's ripple effect has been so humongous that young artists are looking for and pursuing new avenues to learn art. Soon, there will be an initiative coming up known as '*Sarvam* Artists for India' and '*Sarvam* Institute,' which will provide integrated and shackle-free ecosystem to people from all walks of life wanting to get engaged in arts; as Nehha feels that it is very important to connect the dots as fast as possible since nobody knows what happens next.

"For only when we let ourselves be guided by the love of what we do, does life keep us on the path of giving and giving some more."

– Nehha Bhatnagar

Of Artistry in a Sand Grain

Rahul Arya, now a well-known celebrity in the arts field was born and brought up in Delhi like any other common kid. Till class X, he was very good at academics and quite decent in art. During his days at Little Flowers Public Senior Secondary School, he enjoyed participating in a lot of extra-curricular activities and he also used to win a lot of competitions on the similar lines. Drawing, then, was always a hobby for him but he had this perception that one cannot make money by just doing drawing.

The turning point came when he had to leave his school as he could not get into the stream of his choice in class XI. At his new school, going with the flow of students, he took Science with

Computer Science. He used to fail in a lot of subjects about which he is very open and he is still threatened with the deep mysteries of Chemistry. He comments that tuitions after school made him feel like an outcast. He doesn't know how he cleared class XII in the first go itself, scoring a 65%. But he certainly did not enjoy the journey into the realms of Physics, Chemistry and Maths but he thinks that he was pretty decent a student when it came to Computer Science. He always used to believe that this wasn't his calling and hence, he used to spend a lot of time walking alone in the park, contemplating the meaning of life.

Later came the phase of making that big decision—what he actually wanted to pursue. Of course, like everybody else, he was pushed to pursue Engineering. Coming from a family of Civil Engineers and Doctors, he was always scared as everybody used to compare success with the amount of cash in their bank accounts. It took him a lot of courage to confess in front of his parents that he actually wanted to pursue art and that was his actual calling in life.

But his parents found an in-between track and asked him to appear for Architecture exams as it was a combination of Engineering and Drawing and because of his good understanding of drawing he quiet liked the idea what is known as 'engineering drawing.' Due to the same, he was able to clear the most of architecture entrance exams and the entrance exam of National Institute of Fashion Technology. But this wasn't the end of his trauma.

He cheerfully quotes that during the entrance exam of Uttar Pradesh Technical University (UPTU), he drew a big 'R' by using all the optical magnetic reader (OMR) bubbles available on the answer sheet and came back home thinking how creative he was.

He went on to join I.T.S. Engineering College in Greater Noida, Uttar Pradesh, and took up Computer Science Engineering rather than Civil Engineering, since the earlier was way easier for him.

In the first year itself, Rahul says that Chemistry hated him more than he hated Chemistry and this wasn't an easy phase for him...rather, it was one of the most difficult phases of his life.

During one of the exams about global positioning system (GPS) – an important subject in Computer Science Engineering, he had no clue as to what should he write. Then, he dreamt of a beautiful lady with a smartphone in her hand, which was still a big deal back in those days, connected to a satellite revolving around the Earth. Somehow, he got good marks in that paper, enough to clear the same. He kind of proved himself that while it was difficult for him to put his understanding of a GPS satellite into words, but he made his diagram speak for him.

Whenever he used to come home for vacation, he always used to spend the major part of his day drawing something on the windshields of the cars, which were covered with dust. This is where the inner sand artist hidden inside him started to take shape. Somehow or the other, he survived those mentally-challenging days of Engineering.

Even after graduation, he still wanted to pursue arts no matter what, and one of his friends broke to him the news that Indian Institute of Technologies (IITs) were offering a film design course. He had no clue as to what the course was all about, but he still appeared in the entrance exam and got through IIT Bombay.

In his second year at IIT Bombay, he realised that he was never good at what he was pursuing; he was getting a lot of F-R grades which stands for 'fail and repeat.' At this stage of life, he was breaking apart and was embarrassed of himself. He started sketching again and this was his moment of self-awakening.

He took up his first professional project while he was still studying at IIT Bombay. The project was that of a short film titled *Hand VS Sand* and he ended up spending six months on the same which got him an A++ grade and he won a few national awards for the same.

He thoroughly enjoyed working on the project and two months after completing the short film he went ahead and founded the Flying Rocks (FR) Company, which has been named after all the F-R grades that he used to get in IIT Bombay. This is the sole reason why he named his company as the FR Company and by the virtue of the name of his company, he still takes a lot of motivation from his embarrassing days at IIT Bombay. Just for the record, the Flying Rocks Company generated revenue of more than a million rupees in its first year of inception.

According to him, usually engineers pursue something else after they complete graduation and slowly and slowly the society is realising the fact. But art-related fields are still underrated by parents, which need to change as soon as possible.

He recalls that he used to share all his grievances to Piyush Jain, one of his best friends and the guy who pushed him to actually take part in his first television show – *Entertainment Ke Liye Kuch Bhi Karega*. He says one should always remember the people who support them in the hour of need and he thoroughly believes in the ideology of doing what he believes and loves; and that good work should connect to people's heart.

In 2008, he made his own sand-light box and sent it to *Entertainment Ke Liye Kuch Bhi Karega*. A year later, he got a call from Wizcraft to perform live in front of Farah Khan (Indian film director, producer, actress and choreographer) and Anu Malik (Indian music director, singer, actor, director and producer) who were judging the show. He got a lot of appreciation for his work and finally an engineering graduate from a small family had left his mark.

Though his family was still not very supportive about the same, as for them Bollywood and Mumbai meant that letting their son go into a rollercoaster of bad influences.

Afterwards, he started taking this skill of his very seriously and chose the path of becoming a storyteller by the means of sand art. Today, he has successfully completed more than seven hundred shows and more than hundred videos and a lot of them have crossed the million mark as well.

Later, he started being termed as "India's First Sand Artist" and he took on the mission to educate people about the artistic medium. On a fine morning, one of his friends called him and asked him to keep his videos short and precise. That is where he started making time-lapse videos and the concept of storytelling within two hundred seconds was born. On 23rd October,

2013, he uploaded his first two-hundred second sand art video on YouTube. Even after one month of uploading the video, it had not reached the masses, but after a few more days, everybody on the internet started sharing the video and the ripple effect had begun, turning the concept into a brand.

Rahul was and still is very influenced by the King of Bollywood, Shah Rukh Khan (Indian film actor and producer) and therefore he made a video titled *50 Years of SRK in 200 Sec*, which took him approximately two months to make and he uploaded the video online just before the release of *Fan* (Indian film featuring Shah Rukh Khan that released in 2016). In just one hour and thirty-five minutes, the video was shared and retweeted by Shah Rukh Khan himself and later went on to actually break the internet. This gave him a lot of hope and he compares this achievement of his to getting the third prize from of his school principal for the first time. For a student, nothing can be greater than receiving a prize from the head of his institution, and similarly, for Rahul this meant that the man he admired the most in his life had appreciated his work.

He recalls that a popular television channel had earlier rejected him but soon after the *50 Years of SRK in 200 Sec* video started to make rounds all over the internet, he got a call from *Colors* channel to meet Shah Rukh Khan in person on the show *Comedy Nights Bachao*. It was a surprise for Shah Rukh Khan himself to see Rahul making the sketches, live on the show. Rahul also presented a sand art painting of Shah Rukh Khan to him on the show.

Rahul comments that making a sand art animation video is not as easy as it looks because there is no undo command like that in a computer and the frame has to be made from the beginning. Also, a sand artist cannot sweat while making the sand art and use of fans is strictly prohibited. All in all, it is a very complicated and time-consuming procedure but he loves it more than anything else in his life.

His dad was his greatest inspiration whom he recently lost. Every story of his has a message, mostly about how his dad used to see the world. He wishes that there will be one complete day when nothing wrong in the world will happen. He also knows that it's a lot to wish for. Speaking about his family, he says, "It is always a huge support from family and friends, especially my brother. They've shielded me from a few responsibilities when I was working for television shows or events. They are always happy with my television appearances and success, only annoyed with my refusal on getting married for now."

Rahul has never made anything to gain attention. He has always said and worked for what he himself believes in. In his Nepal Tribute video tilted *Nepal will Rise Back from Earthquake*, he asked people to donate when he himself had donated and he also visited Nepal and felt the pain of the victims. He has got several awards including Best Film Award from Carnegie University in the United States of America and from the Film Division of India, to name a few. It makes him proud, but he also has a responsibility that his message should convey both sides of a story. His Peshawar attack tribute video titled *Peshawar School Attack | Maa Sand Art* got humongous success with lakhs of views, even when India and Pakistan were not in good terms, but people in Pakistan welcomed the small sand art tribute with open arms. Hence, if you genuinely believe in your work, it will connect with the heart of the audience.

When asked about his greatest failure in life and how he overcame it, he replies that he considers getting those F-R grades in IIT Bombay as his greatest failure in life up till now; as failing at something you have given your hundred per cent; and something in which you have your heart into, that too after going against all odds. He further added that when viewed from a different perception, that is what gave him the inspiration, motivation and courage to bounce back.

By now, Rahul has been on all the television channels—from *Sony* to *Colors* to *Star Plus* to

CNN IBN to *NDTV India* to *Channel V*—you name it, and he has been there.

"When your loss is big, then your success will be bigger," is something he testifies to and upholds.

India is the land of talents, but being a sand artist is not cakewalk for sure, as depicted by Rahul Arya's story. It requires a great amount of motivation, inspiration and courage to achieve what he has achieved but more than anything, it requires the ability to accept the failures in life and to take them in your pride; not to give up and keep moving in the direction of what one loves doing.

The Piper's Tune

At the tender age of six, Archy Jay could discover that she could sing really well. Since her dad was in the Indian Air Force, Archy used to sing at the Air Force parties and get-togethers. Archy's mom, who was a singer too, used to train her to sing popular Bollywood songs. She recalls how the clapping of the audience at the end of her performances would mean the world to her, because that is what a six-year-old wants!

Even in her schooling days, the 'Archy Jay' was the one-stop for all musical assignments and she was the apple of every teacher's eye when it came to music. But she wasn't equally good at academics. She could only manage to get a mere sixty per cent in her class twelfth board exams, but she has no regrets. For her, the medals that she won at various inter-house and inter-school singing competitions were her biggest achievements. Music is soul to her life and her ambition back then was to be a playback singer or a vocalist.

She quotes, "Everybody wants a Ferrari, but some know the path and others just keep going in the default direction." This is what happened with her as well. She ended up doing Bachelors in Mass Communication from the Asian School of Media Studies as this was the closest she could get to the media industry. Soon, she was occupied full time with the usual proceedings of college and hardly got time to practice music. Though she still had the same dreams and aspirations and had some little fire left in her here and there, she wasn't really happy. Just after completing college, she landed a well-paying job in her brother's multi-national company and would work rigorously like any other corporate employee from 9 am to 5 pm. According to her, she was leading an ordinary life that any present-day youth does after graduating from college.

Her first band known as Rogue Saints, was a metal band that got together to play a few shows, but failed to do any wonders. Archy says that a band is a team and not just a one-man show. She accepts that she was kind of dragging everyone in the band. Though everyone in the band wanted to be a drummer or a guitarist or a vocalist, the problem was that each member of the band had a job which would pay for their expenses. One such incident that Archy shares is that one time the guitarist couldn't reach the venue of the show where he was supposed to play as he was stuck in the traffic jam from Gurgaon (now Gurugram), Haryana to Delhi, after his daily office shift at his corporate company.

Archy has been offered two guitars till now and she already owns two, one of which is an acoustic guitar that was gifted to her on her birthday but she never connected with them. Guitars were never her cup of tea!

She first saw a bagpipe being played by Eluveitie' a popular Swiss folk-metal band from Winterthur, Zurich, and she recalls that her first impression of the bagpipe was like "Fuck! This is so badass!" She was always attracted to doing offbeat things and achieving what seemed unachievable.

As the saying goes, "internet is your first friend," Archy did her research on the internet about bagpipes without wasting any time and soon she was shocked to know how rare and uncommon this instrument was. It did not take her long to figure out that there wasn't a school or a teacher to learn bagpipes from and even quality YouTube videos were hard to find as compared to the present day. But something struck her and she became adamant on getting trained in playing bagpipes. Obviously, the journey to be India's first and only female bagpipe artist wasn't going to be a cakewalk and was filled with failure.

One fine morning, Archy contacted about twenty to thirty bagpipe artists from all over the world from her database which she had made after researching online. One bagpipe artist known as Sean Folsom wrote back to her and went on to become her mentor. He was the first person to guide her. Usually, Sean would send extremely long emails to Archy about various aspects related to bagpipes and Archy would follow. She mentions that bagpipes are different; Hundreds of bagpipe varieties are available across the globe. Even bagpipes are climate dependent and hence, it was getting very difficult for her to narrow down and actually start practicing. But there had to be a way out and soon she bought a chanter, which is one-fourth of a typical bagpipe instrument.

When Archy blew air for the first time into her chanter that her brother got her from Canada, it made pandemonium and it was nowhere near to what she had heard online. Upon this, Archy was really stressed out and heartbroken, but she did not give up. She found a couple of e-books which she would read. It took her a year-and-a-half to complete her first e-book about playing bagpipes because of her tedious job which was still her primary responsibility. Many a times, she would feel the requirement of taking a week off and utilizing that time in doing what she really loved – learning and playing bagpipes.

In 2013, Archy was made the Vice President of an Australian company and she looked after the trade between China and Australia. The company was a subordinate company of her brother's worldwide business empire and was making a decent turnover. Archy would get an in-hand salary of sixty-thousand rupees but somewhere down the line she was feeling suffocated and it was about time that she stepped out of her comfort zone.

She asserts that anybody could be trained to do well in a business because humans have brains that can be easily tamed. She further adds that she has seen a lot of similar examples where people after a time gave up their high-paying jobs because of frustration. She says there comes a time in one's life after which everything becomes unbearable.

Shortly after, she ordered a set of bagpipes from Germany which cost her a whopping one lakh and seventy-thousand rupees that she had saved from her salary. By this time, she had already mastered the art of playing the chanter. The day her bagpipes arrived and she attempted to play it, nothing came out of it. Archy was left shattered as she had already spent around two years learning about them and a huge portion of her savings into it. Her world felt like it was falling apart.

At this point of time her dad came in to console her and told her that being an engineer, he would make her bagpipes work. Well, that is exactly how engineers are! He spent his entire day figuring out what was wrong with the bagpipes but sadly, no sound came out of it. The bagpipes were behaving like a veteran soldier on a protest against the present day government. By now, Archy had started to doubt herself and wanted to give up since she had no teacher to help her out in playing the world's second most difficult instrument.

In February 2014, she got selected for a week-long course to learn bagpipes in Scotland. This also happened to be her first solo international trip and she happily expresses that this was a once in a lifetime opportunity and she did a lot of things which couldn't be done back home in Delhi. Upon arrival, Archy wasn't absolutely bold about it but she came rejuvenated and full of fire. At the same time, she was frustrated as well, because her fingers wouldn't play so fast and she wasn't confident whether people would like the music or not since nobody else played it in India and it was like launching a completely different thing; but she had the courage and confidence that if she put her time into it, everything would go in the right direction.

Finally overcoming the dilemma, in October 2014, she left her job. It was a good, high-paying job and she was high on emotions. She spoke to her parents about the same. They were a little hesitant and unsure at first but later complied with Archy's decision and gave her their full support. Just after leaving the job, she felt like a free bird that was born to conquer new heights and the sky was the limit.

For her first YouTube video titled *The Snake Charmer – Dubstruck (Thunderstruck – AC/DC)*, she got in touch with a film producer who asked her for a lakh with the complete rights over the video and the revenue generated from it. Obviously, that wasn't happening. Later, she got a family friend of hers who worked in MTV to direct her video for only a minimal break even cost of the rent that he had to pay for the filming equipment. For post-production, she contacted one of her close friends who ran a studio and liked Archy's proposal and work and agreed to help her for free. But eventually, he kept pushing the project for weeks. After a few weeks, Archy gave up on him and took the control of the matters in her hand.

Eventually, Archy and her boyfriend started learning Adobe Première Pro and Adobe After

Effects and ended up editing and colour stabilizing the video themselves. Today, the video has more than one hundred and sixty thousand views and has received worldwide appreciation.

In 2015, Archy did another video titled, *Lamb of God Metal Medley (Bagpipes) - The Snake Charmer*. This was the first dubstep version of a rock and roll song which was a completely new rendition and got a lot of hate from the existing supporters of the original song. But Archy was not deterred and went on to do a *Game of Throne Bagpipes Cover*. Today, Archy also known as *The Snake Charmer* has more than six-thousand subscribers on her YouTube channel and the count is growing by the day. The display of her art is not only limited to YouTube, but she also has been playing live at renowned music festivals like *NH7 Weekender*, and *Alt & Pepper* to name a few and has also been featured on *NDTV Goodtimes*.

She has also been featured in British Broadcasting Company (BBC) Radio Scotland and Radio 104.5 frequency modulation (FM). *The Deccan Chronicle* and *The Sunday Guardian* also added a feather to Archy's cap by writing about her in their respective newspapers.

Archy states, "Only you are stopping yourself from success." Absolutely true! She had no teacher and no background playing any other instrument. There were points in her journey where she self doubted herself and thought that leaving her stable paying job was a huge mistake. She had to fight her dreams to keep going. Every day, every video of her gave her a reason to quit. People close to her demoralized her and told her to quit. She trusted people who broke her trust. She has been through various emotional whirlpools and rollercoasters when her beloved bagpipes wouldn't play.

For Archy, every day is an exam. She mentions that failure knocks you on the door to pull you down. According to Archy, India is always a changing scenario and people only get to see the final product and nobody knows the sweat, blood and tears that go into the whole process. "It's all about asking yourself good questions and not the bad ones," she insists.

When jokingly asked about settling down, Archy affirmed that settling down for her means breaking the internet through her YouTube channel; do a bagpipe version of an electronic song; penetrating more into the Indian market and making bagpipes a household name so that people do not get confused between bagpipes and *Bagpiper* whisky; go global with her music; have a music festival of her own in India that would celebrate the spirits of bagpipe artists.

Are you wondering why Archy uses a stage name of *The Snake Charmer*? Well, the reason is that the bagpipes resembles a *Been* or a *Pungi*, a wind instrument played in the subcontinent to attract snakes. By using this stage name, she wants to prove to the world the potential and skills Indian artistes have.

"When you really want to do something, when you're the only hope and you are your only teacher, what do you do? You have no option but to go on."

– Archy Jay

Living *Asimov's* Dream

As a child, Diwakar Vaish, the creator of India's first dancing robot; India's first three-dimensional (3D) printed robot; India's first mind-controlled robot; and the world's first brain-controlled wheelchair used to like breaking things. He always had a curiosity to find out what was inside machines.

Born in Delhi, Diwakar completed his schooling from Bal Bharati Public School (BBPS), Delhi. During primary school—class four and five, he started learning electronics and programming at his dad's institute named *A-SET Training & Research Institute*. Nowadays, this is something that is taught in engineering. During middle school—class six, seven and eight, he was completely into it and his life used to revolve around himself. During senior school—class nine and ten, he opened up and started to go for inter-school events. By now, he was already living a life out of the ordinary.

He wasn't really a kind of academic person. By the time he reached senior secondary school, that is class eleven and twelve; he had already completed all online projects relating to embedded systems. And it was during this time that he got the idea of making a robot. But life had other plans for him!

Senior secondary school is also the time when one has to decide his or her streams that lead to selecting one's career path and it was quite obvious what Diwakar wanted to do in life. He opted for Physics, Chemistry, and Mathematics with Computer Science. But Computer Science usually has the highest cut off followed by Economics, Engineering Drawing and Physical Education. Due to the same reason, the school denied him the course he wanted to study and instead allotted him the medical stream comprising of Physics, Chemistry, and Mathematics with Biology. He went to the then Vice Principal of the school, Mr. Nand Kishore, and told him his story and further challenged him that he could beat any teacher, leave aside the students in school in Computer Science.

But due to its strict policies the school did not move an iota from its already-taken decision.

Diwakar recalls that during his first Biology class, taught by Ms. Meena Malhotra, he kept staring at the white board and thinking what to do. He soon realized that Biology was not his cup of tea and started procrastinating about learning the subject. In a very short period, the first round of cycle tests had begun. On seeing his first-ever Biology paper, Diwakar thought, "What is this piece of shit?" He wrote a few lines and then he went to sleep. He got a few marks in that paper instead of his expectation of a zero. His marks were the least in the class and realizing this, Meena ma'am got furious and dragged Diwakar to the Vice Principal. Diwakar clearly told Mr. Kishore that he did not opt for this subject and he was forced to study Biology.

Soon, the over-hyped class twelve board exams began, and as expected Diwakar, didn't perform well but somehow managed to pass. Diwakar asserts that he always lived by his own rules and that he was very adamant with his vision of robots. He further adds that it is very important for a school to strike a balance between strictness and flexibility.

He started making his first robot during class twelve and later it came out to be known as India's first dancing robot. During the development of the robot, Diwakar did not give any heat to if(s) or but(s). Once the robot was complete, he went to Mr. Laksh Vir Sehgal, Principal of the school to show him his creation. Right there, an amazing gentleman was sitting next to Mr. Sehgal who asked Diwakar what he wanted to do with his robot. Diwakar had no instant answer but after thinking a little he murmured that maybe the robot can be showcased at the upcoming Annual Day function of the school. Mr. Lokesh Bhargava, the gentleman, gave Diwakar his visiting card and told him to contact him two or three days before he wanted to launch his robot.

Diwakar followed the instructions as he was told and Mr. Bhargava, a reporter in The Times of India (TOI), called him to his office and took an interview, which was later published in that week's TOI Sunday Edition. Soon after the interview with TOI, on the same day, Diwakar got a call from Ms. Priyanka who used to work in *Aaj Tak* for an interview. Diwakar told her that he was tired and was heading for lunch and would meet her later. But Ms. Priyanka insisted that he should have lunch at *Aaj Tak* office. By the time he reached *Aaj Tak* office, it was already five-o-clock in the evening and he was informed that he would be interviewed live on *Aaj Tak* that day itself at eight-o-clock for half an hour.

Next morning, he got up a little early at five am than his usual time of seven am. Within a few minutes, a reporter called him that he waiting at the gate of his apartment to take his interview. To which Diwakar responded negatively saying that he will meet the reporter later in the day. But the reporter predicted that Diwakar will not get time later in the day and asked him to get ready as soon as possible. The same day, Diwakar gave a couple of interviews and this tight schedule followed for a week or two. And overnight, he became a national superhero!

When he went back to school to meet the Principal, Mr. Sehgal requested him to teach Robotics to the school children. The one who was denied from taking up the subjects of his choice was now being the opportunity to teach a subject in the same school. Two weeks later after this meeting, Diwakar started teaching students Robotics on Saturdays. Soon, he realized that he cannot do it himself for too long and started hiring a team... and this became the foundation of his own company, which is now known as A-SET Robotics.

Diwakar never wanted to study in India as there was not much scope for research and everyone was more worried about the rat race. He had slept during his All India Engineering Entrance Examination (AIEEE) and had left his answer sheet completely blank. To his surprise, when the result came out, he was ranked at seven lakhs, thirty-seven thousand, three hundred and seventy-three out of twelve lakh aspirants for doing nothing. He though either he would drop a year or start a company. But soon, private colleges started calling him with offers of scholarship. Though it was quite obvious that he would never be able to make it to the top notch, government-run Indian Institutes of Technologies (IITs) or National Institutes of Technologies (NITs) he never wanted to study at these colleges either. On deliberations with Sharda University, they agreed to fund Diwakar's research and were happy to provide him space to conduct his research. After giving a detailed thought, he went on to join Sharda University.

Just after one year, Diwakar got a call from IIT Roorkee for a guest lecture which opened the world of new opportunities for him. Someone who was denied admission into the prestigious IITs on the basis of merit in Indian Institute of Technology – Joint Entrance Examination (IIT-JEE), someone who was still not a graduate was now being called to give a guest lecture at IIT Roorkee. Following the guest lecture at IIT Roorkee, there was a chain reaction and in today, Diwakar serves as guest faculty at IIT Bombay, Kanpur, Roorkee, Kharagpur, Varanasi, Guwahati and Hyderabad; NIT Warangal; Vellore Institute of Technology; Birla Institute of Technology (BIT), Mesra.

Living Asimov's Dream

By now, Diwakar was unstoppable. He went on to create India's first 3D printed robot—*Manav*. *Manav* stands two-feet tall and weighs two kilograms; it is equipped with onboard sound and visual processing so that it can respond to commands. Thanks to the onboard processor and various sensors, he can perform various activities like walking, dancing with the only requirement of human voice commands. He has the capability of binocular vision processing, giving it the ability to perceive depth and perspective. The robot was designed in a span of two months and has a total of twenty-one degrees of freedom, two of which provide the movement of the head allowing it to nod and look around. One degree of freedom goes to the waist which allows it to articulate the waist movement, allowing for a more human-like movement. The robot comes with rechargeable lithium (Li) polymer battery which can keep the robot running for one hour. It is also equipped with Wi-Fi and Bluetooth connectivity and *Manav*'s outer body is made of acrylonitrile butadiene styrene plastic and has been designed completely in A-SET's own 3D printing laboratory in India.

Manav's successor is the world's first brain-controlled wheelchair, which can be used by patients suffering with Locked in Syndrome (LIS). This is a very devastating condition in which the patient loses all his control over the muscles of his body and is not able to move any part of their body. According to Diwakar, it is the responsibility of robotics experts to not only serve the big industries but also to identify and solve the problems faced by people in day-to-day life.

Talking about the wheelchair, Diwakar expresses, "Your wish is its command. To understand its mechanism, our mind is made of millions of neurons and they fire up electrical impulses to the adjacent neurons depending on the thought that has to be produced. The electrical signals that are produced by electrochemical reaction then pass through the brain to the scalp in very minute amounts. These impulses are sensed by a device called an electroencephalogram (EEG) sensor. This electrical signal is firstly amplified and then filtered. These signals are then sent to a system that calculates these electrical signals into meaningful data."

He further adds, "This might sound fairly simple; however, getting the electrical impulse is a very tedious task and then we also need to understand that not everyone's brain is alike. So, if we make one generic program then it might not work for everyone. Therefore, from our prior experience we applied the concept of machine learning (ML) through which we understand how the user's brain functions and then adapts to it automatically. Also, the state of mind changes throughout the day and under different circumstances. Hence, we also need to compensate for the same. As this is a consumer product and not just a lab research, it is our endeavour to make this flawless. We also added various sensors like, temperature sensors, sound sensors and many other sensors to make sure that everything happens just the way it is desired."

Turn up the Torque

Alisha Abdullah from Chennai started her career in sports at the tender age of eight when most girls were busy playing childish games. The daughter of the seven-time racing champion initially started with go-karting. She says that she was super-aggressive as a kid and once, while she was go-karting she lost all her hair as they got entangled in the kart. She adds that she was in massive pain when her dad came and told her to get back inside and ride again. Due to this incident, she was forced to think whether her dad, was really her dad. She went back into the race and actually finished first. Today, when she looks back, she realises that this was something that made a huge difference.

Through out her journey, her dad gave her a lot of courage that nobody else could.

When she was thirteen years old, she used to bunk school, and later, college on a daily basis; just to go to the gym and train as she didn't to get time after her academic pre-occupations. She used to get up in the morning, go to school or college, bunk classes and proceed to the gym to train, come back home, eat food, go to sleep and repeat the schedule the next day.

Alisha got her first superbike at eighteen years. She exclaims that switching between go-karting, the bike and car wasn't an easy thing to do. During her journey, a lot of people around her tried to pull her down. The only thing that made her keep going on and on was her parents. According to her, something of this sort required a lot of sacrifice.

On the track, she used to be a back marker, that is someone who holds a poor rank in a race or is lapped in a race. Usually, her male counterparts used to lead the races. On one such morning, a group of male competitors approached her dad and told him that she did not deserve to be her daughter and that she should sit at home and get married. That day, an emotional Alisha went back home, bolted the door and cried through the night. Later, her mother came and motivated her and boosted her morale by saying she could do what she put her mind to. Following her mother's instruction, Alisha went back to the track to start afresh.

A time came in her career when she met with a catastrophic accident and she was quoted as saying, "In a completely male-dominated sport, I think I bruised quite a few men's egos. They couldn't stand a girl push past guys and many a time they deliberately hit my bike. Being a no-nonsense girl, I always fought back, but the crash was the threshold. I didn't want to race bikes any more, though I loved it," in an interview to *The Times of India* just after the crash.

Alisha says that it's like starting from square one each time she shifted between bike and car racing. She even went abroad to get professional training. She tells that due to her height, bike racing is a little difficult for her when she is turning at a speed of approximately two-hundred and eighty-five kilometer an hour or more, but it all boils down to how much hard work you have put into your sport.

She recently finished in top six at the Toyota Vios Cup 2014 where she competed against fifteen women racers across Asia. Initially, she had thought that being good in India against big boys and men would mean that she was one of the best racers in the world or even Asia to say the least, but this tournament threw her off the hooks and made her realise that she was nowhere in the world standings and that a lot more effort was still required to be put in.

Alisha remarks that the other side of the coin is that she never wanted to be the only individual from India in female motorsport racing and hence, she founded the Alisha Abdullah Racing Academy to guide other talented girls like her. Today, she has created India's first female bike racing team and is simultaneously helping eighty other girls realize their potential and achieve big on the track.

She also mentions that while a single thing in the world can be in your favour, simultaneously hundred things can go against you. She recalls that her journey was not easy at all. Things do look easy from a distance but it's not that simple to go from the worst to the best and to be the leader of the National Car Racing Championship team comprising all males.

Alisha is somebody who self-motivates herself and doesn't require anybody to push herself. She thinks of all those who tried to bring her down, all those who told her that she couldn't do it and those naysayers became her source of motivation. She always wanted to prove everybody wrong—whoever that told her that women couldn't achieve anything in a male dominant sport. All said and done, at the end of the day, she is happy to have proved herself and she exclaims that racing is too much fun for her.

Alisha is on a mission to prove that women are no less. She also strives to encourage women to never give up on their dreams, no matter what; be it in love, life or in career. This is Alisha's message to the present generation.

She imagines her life as a game of football where there is a goal to be reached and she needs to score the goal by going against all odds. She explains that while trying to score a goal, you come across a lot of people who try to bring you down, oppose you and make the chosen path very difficult for you, but one should never give up on his or her dreams. She thinks if she can do it, then every single person on this planet is capable of doing what they love. Everyone is born to do something great and she wants to tell everybody that there's more than to just study, marry, have children and die. Do something in your life so that your own children will call you their role model.

Hands down, Alisha is a role model to all the ladies trying to break stereotypical norms set by our so-called society. She did something many wouldn't think of doing. That is the power of perseverence when you do something you love doing. Alisha is India's first female national racing champion and the first Indian woman to get a podium finish in an international motor sports competition. Well, that's an achievement in itself!

The Notes and Rhythm of Perseverance

Bal Bharati Public School, Pitampura: Delhi boy Varun Rajput was always good in studies and was into sports, especially hockey. He was the captain of his school team for six years. He was super passionate about hockey and represented his school in zonal competitions and also played for Delhi state. Back then, he never took music seriously and liked Physics and Chemistry a lot. Like any other Delhi kid, he followed a very standard path, although he used to sing for his school choir in regular school events.

After completing class XII with a score of 77 per cent, he dropped a year to prepare for

IIT-JEE and realized that he did not want to go to any random college. His parents were always very supportive about him dropping a year. Even today he thinks that dropping a year was a good choice and he has no regrets because this was the year when he picked up the guitar. Now, we know why he never regretted dropping that year!

He had gone to a friend's party where he picked up the guitar and started playing it. After fifteen minutes of playing, he thought that it was something cool and interesting. This was Varun's eureka moment where he realized he had a passion to pursue amidst a mind-boggling year full of Physics, Chemistry and Maths. Later, he requested his parents to buy him a guitar, but his parents were quick to scold him saying, "No nonsense happening!"

One day Varun got his friend's guitar and hid it in his room. When his dad would go to office, he used to take it out and play it for hours. After he was done with his exams, his dad bought him a brand new guitar. By then he had already started understanding the basics of music.

Sadly, he did not get through IITs as he could not clear the individual cut-off for mathematics. But as a Vidyamandir Classes (VMC) student, he was very confident about the subject, so the result came to him as a shocker. Luckily, he got through Delhi College of Engineering (DCE), now

Delhi Technological University (DTU), in 2005 in Information Technology.

Back in the days of VMC, Varun had a friend, Akhil, who used to play the guitar much better than Varun could. Both Varun and Akhil planned on getting into IIT and later forming a band of their own. Akhil got into IIT Delhi and called Varun. Both of them met and a drummer and started jamming. Till that point of the time, Varun only had an acoustic guitar. He soon told his mom that he wanted to buy an electric guitar. Varun used to spend more time in IIT Delhi than at DCE. The best part of being a DCEite was that he did not have to worry about any attendance issues, and because of this, he could practice eight hours a day.

His first band was known as Feedback. As Feedback, they started participating in a lot of competitions and winning a lot of them too. In 2007 and 2008, there was no other band in and around Delhi who could beat them in any competition. Soon, all the guys from IIT Delhi landed up good corporate jobs and it was time for them to move to corporate worlds as all of them were a year senior to Varun. That was a down phase for Varun as what he started came to an end too soon. But this was just the beginning of Varun's troubles.

He already had a failed a paper in the second semester and two papers in the third semester.

Now, in the fourth semester, he had been detained in software engineering. This really threw him off the rhythm of his usual life and what followed was a phase of serious depression, dejection and misery. The placement sessions were not far away and Varun and his friend Gaurav were debarred from the process of campus placement on account of the failed papers and detentions. They could also not clear the minimum academic cut-off placed by various companies. Varun recalls that the whole of their last year of college was pretty bad for him and he used to question him very frequently as to what he would do if he did not get a job.

Varun, along with Gaurav, used to sit outside the training and placement department of DCE and literally used to beg human resource managers of different firms who came to college for placements. Deloitte had allowed them to sit for the aptitude test and both Varun and Gaurav were in the top four candidates selected for the interview, but later both of them were rejected due to insufficient aggregate percentage.

Varun landed his first job as the Senior Professor of Chemistry at Aakash Academy. During his induction session, he went to the blackboard and drew all the music notes and went on to explain how these twelve musical notes made up all the music that is being played around the world, and how similarly all one-hundred and eighteen elements in the periodic table lay the whole foundation of the Chemistry we study. What a bold move! His senior gave him a weird look but that kind of worked; but he was asked to explain something substantial. From his days of VMC, he recalled the mechanisms of Aldol condensation and Canninzaro reaction. Looks like he was good at organic Chemistry!

He studied quite hard in the final year of college and to him it felt like he fucked up his entire life. After graduation, he worked at a start-up for three months after which the start-up had to shut down since he had earlier rejected the offer made by Aakash Academy. Then, he joined Grail Research but couldn't stand the work. After his stint at Grail Research, he went on to join Corporate Consultant Board (CCB) as a Management Consultant. He got promoted in the first year of his service at CCB. He worked there for three years; and in total, by now, he had already spent around five years switching between different jobs but neither the work nor the paychecks could lure him.

By mid-2012, he realised that music had been missing from his life for more than two years now and there was a void in his life which could only be filled with music. Soon, Varun and another friend Mridul had started a tech start-up. Varun also started playing guitar once again during this period. He pitched to Mridul, a fellow guitarist, but he was apprehensive about forming a band. Within a month, Varun had written three songs and *Antariksh*, the popular Hindi rock band had started to take shape. Varun once again pitched to Mridul and this time he agreed, but with a clause that they would give Antariksh six-month probation period before making a final decision. Varun, on hearing this, was very happy though he knew that everything was time-bound. Though this limitation of time pushed them to achieve more in the little they had.

Without wasting any time, both of them auditioned a few drummers and Vipul came into the picture. Antariksh's debut song *Dheere Dheere* was a big experiment and these guys used to practice about ten to twelve hours a day. The song was launched in January 2013 and slowly people started appreciating it and the song got popular. This triggered the work towards their first album *Khoj*.

Within less than a year, *Antariksh* launched its first album with eleven songs. This was also a turning point in Varun's journey as Mridul had come up to him and said that if music becomes work for him, he couldn't really tolerate it and at some point of time he wanted to return to the US; so he thought of quitting the band and all the money that Varun had made from his corporate jobs had begun to dry up as the band was making no money at that point of time.

The days of struggle were back and Varun had to reach out to colleges in search of opportunities. There was very less or almost negligible organic reach, but Varun was very clear about the vision of the band and never wanted to get famous and he did not have the slightest of doubt about the latest product of the band.

Raghav joined the band in March 2014 and soon left it to co-found Chaayos. Gloomy days were back in Varun's life and he was the only one left in the band and nothing was changing on the band's front, and by this time, he too had exhausted almost all his monetary resources. He had almost given up on the band and went into a weird mental zone, but life had some other plans for Varun and Antariksh.

Few months after on 31st December 2014, Antariksh got its first paid gig. The second paid gig happened in January 2015, followed by the third, fourth and fifth gig in February, the same year. Things had just started to fall in place and the band had started making money – a lot of it. Varun remarks that March 2014 was like the gestation period of the band and at this point of time, Mridul had finally left the band and the lead singer of the band was gone.

But Varun did not look back since then and he exclaims that it has been a rollercoaster journey going up and down, which is synonym to people joining and leaving the band but what remained constant is this guy – Varun Rajput!

The three most excruciating phases of Varun's life till now had been the year after class XII when he dropped out; failing and getting detained in semester examinations; and Antariksh's phase after *Khoj*.

Now Antariksh is a well-known and popular Hindi rock band that has garnered international acclaim. A couple of Antariksh's achievements are as follows:

- Rated by MTV as one of the best Hindi rock bands in the country.
- Featured on Season 4 of *Music Mojo* on Kappa TV.
- Selected as the only band out of 167 Indian bands to play and share the stage with Farhan Akhtar (Indian film director, screenwriter, producer, actor, playback singer, lyricist and television host), Rekha Bharadwaj (Indian playback singer), Sachin Tendulkar (former Indian cricketer and captain), Arvind Kejriwal (Indian politician and the current Chief Minister of National Capital Territory of

Delhi), Leander Paes (Indian professional tennis player)' and various other eminent personalities at *India Today Mind Rocks*.

- The band's first single, *Dheere Dheere* got nominated for VIMA Asia Awards.

The second album of the band is due to be out anytime soon and now Varun's parents are quiet supportive of him being in the music industry and he jokingly remarks that if he even thought of leaving Antariksh right now, his parents would literally throw him out of their house.

Somebody rightly said that timing, perseverance and ten years of trying would eventually make you look like an overnight success. Even though after failing so much almost at each point of his life, Varun Rajput never gave up on his dream and kept on putting endless efforts no matter what happened into something that he loved. Today, he is truly an inspiration to the youth of the country and he is a perfect example of somebody who celebrated his failure to convert it to success. Keep doing what you love, Varun!

Blue Streak

In a country which is obsessed with cricket, surprisingly few women have taken up this sport. Sadly, not everyone in this country knows about Mithali Dorai Raj, the female counterpart of Virat Kohli, captain of the Indian cricket team. She has indeed challenged this convention to become the pioneer of women cricket in India.

A true sportsperson and an inspiration for many currently, she leads the Indian women's cricket team and is the second-highest run scorer in international cricket. That's not all; she is also the second woman cricketer to surpass the five-thousand run benchmark.

Here are some excerpts from the Indian skipper:

On Becoming a Cricketer

"It was my parents who put me into cricket. I have been questioning them myself, 'Why put me into sports?' They say it was because I was too lazy. They are right, actually."

"I hated cricket initially as I was not keen to take up sports. I was already pursuing Bharatanatyam then; it was my dad's initiative to turn me into a professional cricketer. I have spent all my childhood and growing up years pursuing this sport. It has become a way of living now and I have come to a point in my career that I have started to enjoy it."

"I learnt dance for eight years. Cricket happened by chance. I tried to manage both for a few years, but it was getting difficult."

"It started with my brother. He used to play cricket in school. Actually, when I was young, I used to go with my father where he practiced. I used to stand outside the ground, and returned the ball when it came my way. That was how it started. When I was eight, I went on a summer vacation where I was the only girl. Naturally, they all played cricket, and being the only girl, I got preference when it came to batting. I later played with the boys in the nets, which helped me hone my skills."

On Reaction of Relatives

"When I started playing cricket, it didn't go down too well with my relatives. My grandparents didn't want me to pursue cricket. I was a classical dancer, but cricket was what I enjoyed the most. The fact that I played the boy's game didn't go down too well with my family members but my parents were very supportive. Things got worse when I used to attend family gatherings as everyone would look at me differently. But once I started establishing myself in the sport, people took notice and things started changing."

On Alternate Career Options

"I would have been in civil services. Though I loved Bharatanatyam and pursued it quite seriously, I would have loved to get into the civil services."

On Sacrifices Made by Parents

"They have sacrificed a lot to give me everything that I needed in my early years as a cricketer when there was no money and sponsorship to buy cricket equipment or to go on tours. I hail from a middle class family. Both my parents were working but mom had to quit her job to cater to the demands of the game like picking and dropping me at training sessions. My dad had to forgo his promotion as a banker because that would mean he had to shift his base and that wasn't good for my cricketing career."

On Comparing Men's and Women's Cricket

"Let's face it. To imagine women's cricket on par with men's cricket is a little too farfetched. In India, we have a long, long way to go before it can happen. There are too many things to be done to get to that level. Most importantly, we need to win games. And to have a winning team, there are a lot of other factors that come into play."

On Evolution of Women's Cricket

"Regarding the standards of the game, yes, it has evolved. There was a time when one hundred and fifty runs on the board would be a decent total, but now, teams have started scoring somewhere in between two hundred and fifty runs to three-hundred runs on many occasions."

On Losing in World Cup

"It's not like we are not doing well, but we are failing in major tournaments. With the World Cup happening in India, it was a brilliant opportunity for us to do very well, but we as a team, for whatever reason, could not click. We didn't even qualify for the Super Six. That was a big disappointment."

On Domestic Cricket

"There is a huge need for more tournaments at the domestic level. Our domestic program runs for around two months and if we are to be the world's best we must have more tournaments throughout the year. Holding camps is fine, but match practice is equally important for the betterment of women's cricket in India."

On Being the Captain of the Team

"As a captain I have an added responsibility. Firstly, I need to be good with people management as I have to deal with a variety of people in the team. Captaincy has its own pressure, but more than anything it is a huge honour. Very few privileged ones get to lead India at the highest level. As a captain I need to be the best at all given time, just not on the playing field but off the field too, as I am the ambassador and representative of our country. The players look up to the captain at all times to motivate and inspire them, so it's imperative that I inspire and lead them by example."

On Challenges Faced

"I don't think there is anything that has been like a constant challenge to me, but yes, one issue that has always been a challenge is that each time

I go in, people always expected me to score runs. When you set a standard of being consistent over a period of time, people tend to expect inhuman things from you. And sometimes, players need to be allowed to be themselves."

"Other challenges are of performing and injures too. There was a time when I thought of quitting cricket because of an injury. It was playing a lot on my mental side as well at one point. I would give a lot of credit to the physiologists. Because of their efforts in keeping me fit and treating me time and again, and sometimes even motivating me to not quit helped me continue. That's very crucial as some injuries take a long while to heal and some are career threatening, but then you need to have good people around you to motivate you."

On Mental Conditioning

"Mental growth is as important as skill. As a younger player, you give more time to moulding yourself as a skilled player. But when you start playing at a higher level, that's when it comes into play. It becomes important then if you are strong under pressure that you can take other pressures. You need to be mentally strong and that's when your skill will enhance after a certain stage. We follow certain things from the time we start playing and it becomes a habit. Sometimes it's a person's nature and sometimes you work on some things. It's my nature to be very quiet and calm. I don't let out any emotions. I am not very expressive. So, it's very difficult for the opposition or others to read what I am thinking or going through. At the same time, I have made an effort to work on my mental aspect by challenging myself in the net sessions because that's when we can work on these things which will help us at the competition stage. Also, I speak to my dad on how to prepare myself for during pressure situations because he knows me as a daughter and as a player and is in a better position to guide me."

On Team Culture

"When I made my debut, I was the only kid in the team. Almost everyone else was nearly double my age, which meant I had to reach out to them. A lot of the youngsters these days are of the same age-group. They enjoy themselves together, but we talk among ourselves a lot as well. On the ground, of course, we are all equals and professionals. The culture has also changed. Back then there was a certain difference between the seniors and juniors. You, as a kid, could not go and put your arm around the shoulder of a senior. These days we are more casual and friendlier."

On What She Loves About Batting

"What I enjoy most—I think it's the uncertainty of the sport as well as batting. Today you score a hundred and tomorrow you end up scoring zero; it's like you are not very certain about things and that's something which is very endearing about it. When I bat I am in a completely different zone. The outside world doesn't exist for me then. I feel it's something like a zone where I am very peaceful and calm. Even if I am pretty occupied in my mind with certain issues that I have, I am used to blocking it off when I walk in to bat. It's something like a peaceful place, though the challenges are quite different; but that's something I enjoy."

On Sledging

"Women's cricket is not as aggressive as men's cricket. There is no abusive language or bad talk. It's more of competitive cricket. There is aggressive body language, but no sledging."

On Media Coverage

"There were times when we hardly had any media coverage. But it all changed after we won the Asia Cup in 2008. Suddenly, the media woke up and noticed our achievement. We got good coverage, and I am glad that it's a different scenario now. People now know that women's cricket exists."

"People not aware of women's cricket are ignorant purely because the matches are not televised. More the matches that are aired, better the awareness that spreads for the sport."

On Fan Following

"To be honest, I don't really get attention the same way that the men's team gets from their female fans."

On Being Lazy

"I am a very laidback person, and I must say cricket hasn't changed this attitude of mine even a bit. I love to sleep and am a very easy-going person."

On Winning the Prestigious Padma Shri Award

"Well, it was totally unexpected. I was pitted against Virat Kohli and I did not think initially that I would have any chance of winning the award. I'm really grateful to the Government of India for recognizing my services to Indian cricket. I'm confident that such awards will motivate the youngsters taking up women's cricket."

On Being the Second Batswoman to Score Five-thousand Runs in One-day Internationals

"Statistics never interested me, but in sports they hold a far bigger value. I feel happy that I am the first Indian and the second in the world to achieve that milestone. It reflects my consistency and I am happy that my dad is proud of my achievements."

On Talent in India

"There is no paucity of talent in the country. India has a huge population and talented youngsters are always going to come up through the ranks. The point is, if we have more domestic tournaments, then the youngsters will gain experience quickly and be international material in a year or so, whereas when you have lesser domestic tournaments, these youngsters will take three-four years to gain experience and handle the pressures of international cricket."

On How Long She Will Play Cricket

"A lot depends on my how my body shapes up."

On the Future of Women's Cricket in India

"As a captain I feel that with these new formats introduced by the ICC we have more matches in a year. This team of young girls has been doing well in the last two years and I am hoping that by 2017 we should be in a good position to take up the challenges and pressure of the World Cup and do much better than the last one. As a senior, I find a lot of talent in these young girls. It's just a matter of matches. Of late we have been playing a lot of matches which will keep us in good stead."

On Today's Children

"For children of today I would advise whatever field they choose they have to give time to grow and not hurry to get overnight success. The old saying goes; 'there is no substitute to hardworking and individual sacrifices as they reflect your priority.' Success demands sincerity and perseverance at every stage."

On Her Journey as a Cricketer

"It has been a long journey; from the time I represented India in 1999 till 2016. There have been a lot of ups and downs and a lot of challenges, but I would say it's been good. There have been some memorable moments during my career so far, like winning the Test. In 2005 we finished as the runners-up in the International Cricket Council (ICC) World Cup and a disappointment like in the 2013 World Cup when we couldn't make it into the Super Six. But all said and done, it has been a wonderful journey."

The Tree of Knowledge

Kunal Arora, the co-founder of The Education Tree (TET) learned the meaning of failure when he scored a 'whopping' fourteen marks out of a hundred in Mathematics in the All India Senior School Certificate Examination (Class XII) by the Central Board of Secondary Education. For Kunal, an alumnus of Bal Bharati Public School, Rohini, Delhi, this little *tête-à-tête* with failure changed his life completely.

Overall, he had managed a fairly-decent aggregate of 73.7 per cent, which allowed him to get into Ram Lal Anand College of the University of Delhi, but it did not allow him to migrate to the college of his preference due to his compartment in the Class XII exams. Back then, the college did not have any theatre society. So, Kunal pledged to start one himself, and today, the dramatics society that Kunal started is popularly known as *Hasratein*.

Next year, he was introduced to English literature at Shri Guru Tegh Bahadur Khalsa College of the University of Delhi, when he started to question everything from whether he needed a full-time job to the kind of money he wanted to earn in life. His parents always wanted him to become an Indian Administrative Services officer or at least take up a government job as it was and still is considered a stable and secure job, at least in India.

Kunal says, "All failures up till now came together to start something new, something that would add value to a student's lives." But sadly, he did not know what he wanted to do. Hence, he remarks that he even failed miserably to start something of his own. Finally, he started a volunteer-based youth club which was perceived as another college-based society and not a start-up that wanted to disrupt the education sector.

He remembers that once he went to a big brand's corporate office to secure funding and the officer there liked the idea, but told him to return with his boss. At that point of time, he needed funds badly and therefore went back to the same office. This time he was asked, "Aren't you the same guy? Did I not tell you to come with your boss?" Thank God, this time Kunal told the officer that he was the Chief Executive Officer (CEO). He was rejected yet again.

He recalls that nothing worked for him. The society always questioned him for what he was doing; everybody put him down. For him, it has been a heck of a bumpy ride. He then hit-rock bottom when he failed to convince people to even be a part of what he had created. Reaching out to people wasn't as big a task as convincing them to join *The Education Tree*, which was of utmost importance, but nobody was ready to see the change that Kunal wanted to bring.

Initially, Kunal got huge amounts of rejection from his parents and friends. By now, he had started to take double amounts of cash from home, which he used to completely bootstrap *The Education Tree*. Lately, he had no time to have food or anything else in life. Kunal states, "Me and my team did not know what we were doing. We had an idea but no direction. But I always wanted to do some constructive work in the education sector that would create a space for young people where they were allowed to do whatever they wished to." On the other hand, he was given a failure stamp and if *The Education Tree* failed to reap its magic, then it would have been a pretty explosive combination.

Simultaneously, he also started organising and performing in his school's annual function and alumni meet. In 2014, he enrolled himself in a Master of Arts in Mass Communication course and after that he went on to do a diploma in International Business. He felt that a lot of time was being wasted and thought that he would involve himself in something constructive.

Kunal believes that in nine to five jobs people sit idle for hours, but still get paid at the end of the month, whereas entrepreneurship is very funny. For example, to get funds, the founders keep questioning and doubting themselves as if they are doing something wrong.

To add to Kunal's suffering, one of the biggest dilemmas of his life revealed itself – to take up the offer made to him by Zomato, a restaurant search, discovery and food-ordering platform. He had cleared the final interview round and was going to be paid a hefty amount to work at Zomato's Gurugram office. At that point of time, *The Education Tree* had no cash inflow, but Kunal chose do what he loved and make money out of it.

When quizzed about the problems of the Indian Education System, Kunal comments that, "In a workshop, when kids are asked to draw houses; seventy-five per cent or more end up drawing huts whereas nobody these days lives in huts, at least the urban area from where these kids belong to." He further adds, "The system is such that, it relies on set images and a constructive noise is considered as chaos. Out of a total of forty-five periods in a week, only two are reserved for physical education and one for library; an alarming situation indeed."

According to him only nineteen per cent time is given for extra-curricular activities, which helps to shape the overall persona of a student. "I have never used the Pythagoras Theorem in my entire life and I am still waiting for that day to come," is one of his famous dialogues you'll hear him saying on many occasions. He quotes, "The growth of the students of this generation is stagnant. Everybody is considered similar and is being taught exactly the same thing and as a result, the diversity of the biggest democracy of the world is being neglected. According to the Constitution of India, sex education and legal awareness about the same are mandatory," exerts Kunal.

The Education Tree, which at one time had to give a big deal even to get one application, now gets over fifty-thousand applications only from students studying in Delhi and the National Capital Territory in a year. It holds 'The Youth Leadership Summit,' a three-day residential conference, wherein a person is celebrated for his or her individuality. They go through a set of workshops and sessions, aimed at transforming him or her into a visionary leader. Another such conference is the 'Meet Your Self' conference which focuses on self-development.

This is just a beginning of an era for *The Education Tree* and the team behind it including Kunal and Smriti Singhal, director and co-founder of *The Education Tree* whom Kunal had met while pursuing his bachelor's degree. If both of them had given up early in their lives to failures, then India's most dynamic youth organisation today would not have been created. It's true that to achieve something big in life, you have to compromise a little, even if the pain is temporary.

Well, it's a sheer story of brilliance: how Kunal celebrated numerous failures that he encountered on his way by staying true to his cause and more importantly, doing what he loved the most. Biz Stone, co-founder of Twitter, Obvious, Medium and Jelly rightly said, "Timing, perseverance and ten years of trying will eventually make you look like an overnight success."

Epilogue

After reading all the chapters, you might have realized that though all the individuals belong to different fields of life and that they all have a different meaning or perception of failure; yet they have something in common—something that sets them apart, something that makes them the epitome of success in their respective fields.

How do we explain when things don't go as we assume or expect them to? Or better, how do we explain when others are able to achieve things that seem to defy all of the assumptions? As it turns out, there's a pattern. As it turns out, all the great inspiring leaders and organizations in the world, all think, act and communicate the exact same way. And it's the complete opposite to everyone else. Why? How? What? Every single person, every single organization on the planet knows what they do, hundred per cent. Some know how they do it, whether we call it our differentiated value proposition or our proprietary process or our unique selling point. But actually, very few people or organizations exactly know why they do what they do. None of what is written here is my opinion. It's all grounded in the tenets of biology.

Not psychology, biology. People don't buy what we do; they buy why we do it. If we talk about what we believe, we attract those who believe what we believe. This is a very famous concept known as *The Golden Circle* by Simon Sinek. The goal is not to build relations with everybody who need what we have. The goal is to build relations with people who believe in what we believe in too. The goal is not just to work with people who are willing to work; it's to work with people who believe in what we believe.

Whether, it was Anupama or Arunabh; Nehha or Rahul; Archy or Diwakar; Alisha or Varun; Mithali or Kunal, whatever they achieved in life was because they knew why they were doing what they were doing and for the same reason no failure could deter them from their end goal.

Writing about them reminds me of Steve Jobs' famous quote:

"Here's to the crazy ones, the misfits, the rebels, the troublemakers, the round pegs in the square holes. The ones who see things differently—they're not fond of rules. You can quote them, disagree with them, glorify or vilify them, but the only thing you can't do is ignore them because they change things. They push the human race forward, and while some may see them as the crazy ones, we see genius, because the ones who are

crazy enough to think that they can change the world, are the ones who do."

While reading the book, did you ever by chance contemplate on what is that one most important thing that sets these individuals a class apart? Well, they all did what they loved doing. According to the National Employability Report 2013, forty-seven per cent of graduates in India are not employable in any sector of the knowledge economy and the percentage for Engineers and Masters of Business Administrations (MBAs) graduates is even worse. We all have our unique calling, but we mostly kill it because we are more concerned about what society will think about us.

If Anupama, Arunabh, Nehha, Rahul, Archy, Diwakar, Alisha, Varun, Mithali or Kunal had listened to society or had chosen their careers according to societal norms and expectations, then hands-down, today they would have been in a pretty bad rat race slogging for thirty days, working from nine to five at a desk in a corporate job for just a pay check to be spent on drinks on a Friday night. But instead, they chose to do what they loved the most—something that motivates them enough to get out of bed each morning, whether it's a weekday or weekend. Work for them does not feels like work; and this is what gives them enough courage to get back on their feet each time after life knocks them down.

Maybe, just maybe, the greatest successes come from having the freedom to fail.

Trust me, many of these individuals do not make hefty amounts of money till date or did not make until a short while ago; But for them, their why, their cause, their core values matter much more than anything else, specifically money. For them, money is just a secondary outcome of what they love doing. At the same time, they are sure that they'll never face a time when there would be financial crunches because they are getting paid to play!

The problem with the present generation, popularly known as Millennials (also known as Generation Y) is that they erroneously assume to know why they are doing what they are doing; however, everybody is focused on making an impact in the times of instant gratification without realizing that leaving a long-lasting impact requires patience, perseverance and celebrating failure. Making or leaving an impact is an outcome and not a cause or a factor of motivation. Millennials, including me, at times, while trying to make an impact, forget what they actually loved doing. If each one of the individuals talked about in this book wanted to make an impact as an artiste or as a robot researcher or as a woman in the armed forces or as an entrepreneur or as sportsperson, then they would not have achieved the respective levels of success that they are at today.

Epilogue

It wouldn't be wrong to draw the following conclusions from the stories of these brilliant minds:

1. Do what you love.
2. Believe in yourself so strongly that the world cannot help but believe in you too.
3. Step out of your comfort zone.
4. Take risks. If you win, you'll be happy. If you lose, you'll be wise.
5. Jump off a cliff and build a plane on the way down.
6. Start where you are. Use what you have. Do what you can.
7. Focus on the solution, not on the problem.
8. Live a few years of life most people won't, so that you can spend the rest of your life like most people can't.
9. Perseverance and years of hard work would make you look like an overnight success.
10. Celebrate failure.

We all are amazing. You. Me. Everyone. The only thing is, we have to find it. Discover it. Find out, what is that we are amazing at. It could be anything. Writing. Talking. Cooking. Jumping. It doesn't matter. Some people are amazing at nothing. It's the pursuit that makes it worth it. Curiosity of what do we like? What do we

Epilogue

hate? What can we adjust to? And what can we adapt? There's no right answer. There's no wrong answer. There's just the amazing. And the constant pursuit of it. It is this curiosity that we need to tickle. It is this curiosity that we have to fuel. It is this curiosity that will help us grow by leaps and bounds.

To sum it up one last time, I had a great enriching experience during the holistic development of the book. And one of my greatest learning from writing the book is that the meaning of failure for different bunch of people is different. There were times during the production of the book when I wanted to quit writing, but then, I would come back to the chapters written here for re-motivating myself.

To say the least, keep doing what you love and celebrate failure. May failure be with you!

✹ ✹ ✹

I hope the book added some value, even if a little, to your life and that I did enough justice to the whole idea of 'celebrating failure.'

If you liked the book, kindly pass it on to someone who you think would believe in the ideology of 'celebrating failure' as much as you do.

✹ ✹ ✹

Epilogue

This is your life. Do what you love, and do it often. If you don't like something, change it. If you don't like your job, quit. If you don't have enough time, stop watching television. If you are looking for the love of your life, stop; they will be watching for you when you start doing things you love. Stop over analysing, all emotions are beautiful. Life is simple. When you eat, appreciate every last bite. Open your mind, arms and heart to new things and people; we are united in our differences. Ask the next person you see what their passion is, and share your inspiration dream with them. Travel often; getting lost will help you find yourself. Some opportunities only come once, seize them. Life is about the people you meet, and the things you create with them so go out and start creating. Life is short. Live your dream and share your passion.

– The Holstee Manifesto

References

A LITTLE *QTIYAPA* NEVER HURT ANYONE

- Youth Ki Awaaz: www.youthkiawaaz.com/2016/07/the-viral-fever-arunabh-kumar
- MensXP: www.mensxp.com/culture/people/31886-how-arunabh-kumar-made-tvf-a-bigger-cult-than-mtv-and-even-beat-netflix-to-the-online-television-race.html
- Your Story: www.yourstory.com/2013/10/arunabh-kumar-qtiyapa

BLUE STREAK

- The Times of India: www.timesofindia.indiatimes.com/news/I-was-asked-to-choose-between-love-and-cricket-Mithali-Raj/articleshow/30996942.cms
- Board of Control for Cricket in India: www.bcci.tv/news/2015/features-and-interviews/9640/the-wonderful-journey-called-mithali-raj
- Cricket Country: www.cricketcountry.com/articles/mithali-raj-when-it-comes-to-pure-cricket-skill-women-are-at-par-with-men-461590

- Sportskeeda: www.sportskeeda.com/cricket/people-looked-at-me-differently-because-i-played-cricket-mithali-raj
- Brain Feed Magazine: www.brainfeedmagazine.com/interview-indias-pride-mithali-raj

EPILOGUE

- TED Talk (How Great Leaders Inspire Action by Simon Sinek): https://www.ted.com/talks/simon_sinek_how_great_leaders_inspire_action
- The Holstee Manifesto: https://www.holstee.com/pages/manifesto

Acknowledgement

"Every person is a new door to a different world."

– Anonymous

Somebody had rightly said that each person we meet teaches us something new, something different.

First of all, I would like to thank my parents Dr. Avdhesh Kumar and Dr. Usha Goel, for if they would not have been so strict with me, I would not have ventured out of my comfort zone as much as I have done now. Being a rebellious kid at home helped me see my environment in a totally different light and this helped me create enriching and meaningful experiences—like the one in your hand—for people who admire me, and most importantly, for myself.

A big shout to Rohan Thapar and Nehha Bhatnagar for being such an amazing support and for tolerating my weird mood swings (basically, me!) and subsequent piles of calls, messages and mails. Another friend that is noteworthy of appreciation is Manasa Saikumar. She came to my rescue on random days with her positive vibes when I used to feel like killing the book.

Acknowledgement

This book wouldn't have been possible without the constant support of Anupama Joshi, Nehha Bhatnagar, Rahul Arya, Archy Jay, Diwakar Vaish, Alisha Abdullah, Varun Rajput, Kunal Arora, Wioleta Burdzy Seth and Archana Sardana.

My warm wishes to the team at Notion Press whom I had been pestering the last few months. I believe I'd left no stone unturned in driving them nuts.

You would be happy to know that this book has been crowd-funded and this could not have been possible without the support of those who put their immense belief in me and the book. I will always be in debt to you for your support in a time of need. A special mention for all my friends who donated small amounts of money—which is still a huge and significant part of their pocket money—by curtailing their monthly expenditures. You guys; you are a whole lot of wonderful people! A complete list of the contributors can be found at the end of the book. I am also grateful to the people who did not make it to the list since they wanted to remain anonymous and have taught me an important lesson about the power of giving in life.

Last but not the least, this is for Sonakshi Kothary; She stood by me during the worst of times when nobody else did and hugged me

Acknowledgement

tightly when I had lost all hopes of coming out of the cyclone named life. She is the only individual who is allowed to call me something as personal and endearing as "*Dhruvieee Puvieeeeee*" (which is actually not as annoying as it may sound!).

Sorry, if I missed someone by chance. I have immense respect and love for all of you for having believed in me and in my values. Even more respect and love for those who tried to pose a hurdle in my way during the development of the book. Well, the book is all about celebrating failure! Isn't it?

Lots of love.

drops the mic

Contributors

Usha Goel and Avdhesh Kumar
Srinavasa Rao
Prateek Chhabra
Shivangi Gupta
Wioleta Burdzy and Kamal Seth
Surbhi Samra
Rohan Thapar
Manasa Saikumar
Puneet Malhotra
Deepshikha
Udit Mongia
Shivani and Keshav Sethi
Priya Taneja
Komal Gupta
Jaytirth Ahya
Anwesha Bandyopadhyay
Vishesh Khakhar
Meghdut Roy Chowdhury
Tanya Gupta
Rakhi Naik
Srishti Gupta
Priya Varshney
Abhay Kumar Mishra

*And a lot of anonymous contributors as well.

About the Author

Brain of a techie, yet heart of an artist!

Dreamer. Believer. Innovator.

Dhruv follows curiosity over passion and he loves to make friends with stress. A chain reaction is what drives him crazy and beware, he asks tons of questions. Moreover, he personally believes in the idea that there is no scheduled time for anything and magic happens when we step out of our comfort zone. The motto of his life is to do what he loves and hence be happy!

To read more about the author, log on to dhruvavdhesh.net.

www.ingramcontent.com/pod-product-compliance
Lightning Source LLC
Chambersburg PA
CBHW031429210526
45464CB00005B/2120